NEWCASTLE IN PHOTOGRAPHS

SIMON McCABE

AMBERLEY

First published 2022

Amberley Publishing
The Hill, Stroud
Gloucestershire, GL5 4EP

www.amberley-books.com

Copyright © Simon McCabe, 2022

The right of Simon McCabe to be identified as the Author of this work has been asserted in accordance with the Copyrights, Designs and Patents Act 1988.

ISBN 978 1 3981 0632 1 (print)
ISBN 978 1 3981 0633 8 (ebook)

British Library Cataloguing in Publication Data.
A catalogue record for this book is available from the British Library.

Typesetting by SJmagic DESIGN SERVICES, India.
Printed in the UK.

INTRODUCTION

One of my favourite features of Newcastle is its extraordinary blend of the old and new; the way Georgian stone, medieval cobbles and new millennium glass all stand gloriously in harmony. It was my aim to capture this contrast.

During my time photographing, the world had been hit by the Covid-19 pandemic and the once bustling streets of Newcastle were stripped bare.

I realised that, as well as capturing the city's contrasting buildings, I could capture this new disparity.

I hope you enjoy seeing Newcastle in this way – especially now we're enjoying its thriving return. For reassurance, social distancing and PPE guidelines were adhered to while photographing.

ABOUT THE AUTHOR

Simon McCabe is a Teesside-based photographer whose photography journey started over fifteen years ago. A close family member who was no longer able to travel said, 'Travel the world and take as many photos as you can, so I can see and experience the world through your eyes.' Since then, his experience, style and passion has been evolving and with each new challenge he has learnt new techniques in photography and editing. Nature, landscape and wedding photography are his main fields of experience.

Which of my photographs is my favorite? The one I'm going to take tomorrow.

Imogen Cunningham

Facebook: SimonMcCabePhotography
Instagram: Simonmccabe5
Email: Simon.mccabe2@gmail.com

Autumn in Old Eldon Square

Beehive, Cloth Market

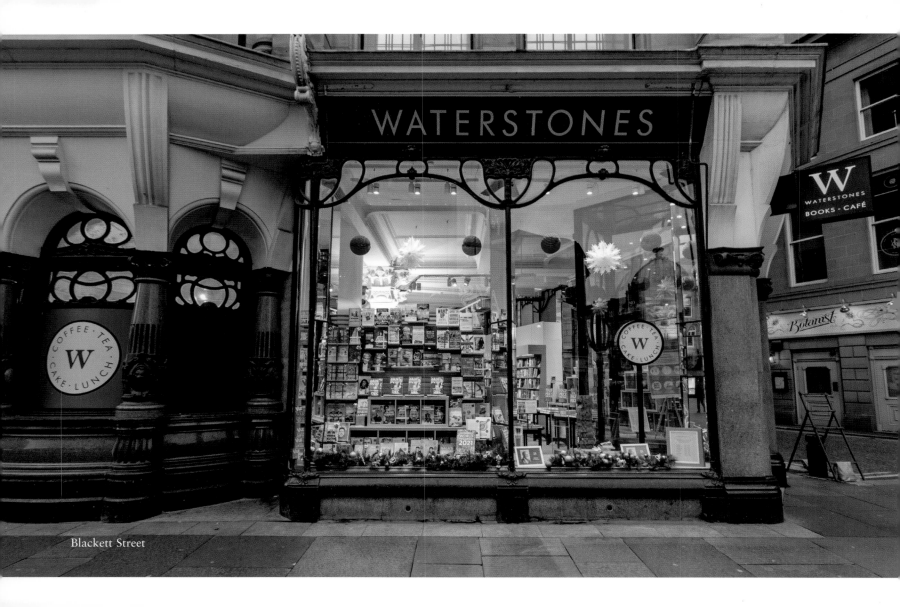

WATERSTONES

BOOKS · CAFÉ

Blackett Street

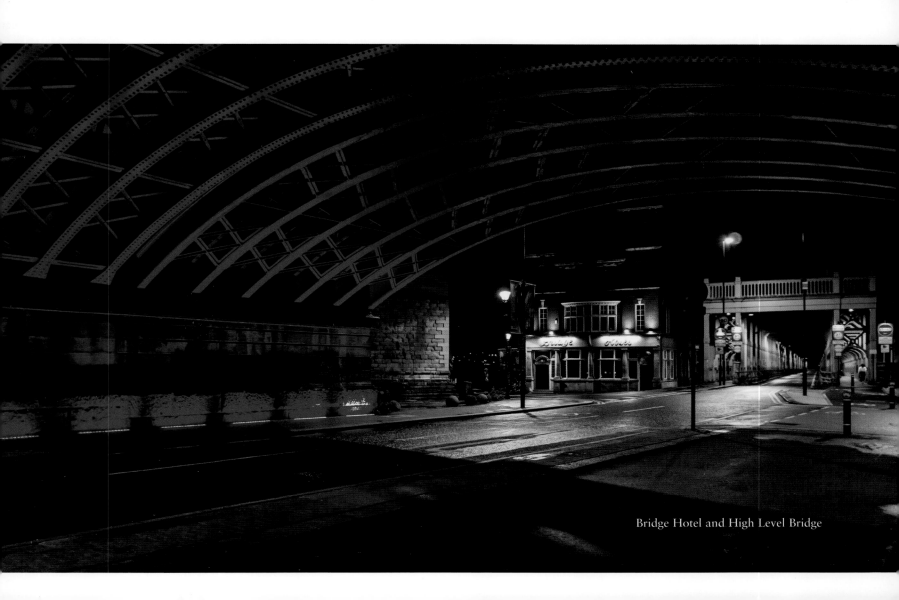

Bridge Hotel and High Level Bridge

Central Arcade

Castle view, Central station

Central station

Chimney pots, Newcastle

China Town, New Year 2020

Chinatown Arch

Christmas market,
Northumberland Street

Christmas market

The West Walls and the newest skyscraper, Hadrian's Tower

Dean Street at night

Dean Street in lockdown

Delivery in motion

Eldon multistorey car park

Eldon Square, Northumberland Street

Eldon Square reflections

Entrance to Eldon Square from Grey's Monument

Forth Street arches

THE HANCOCK MUSEUM

Great North Museum: Hancock

Hampton by Hilton, Newcastle

Haymarket

High Bridge Street

Acorn Road, Jesmond

Autumn street view, Jesmond

Dean Armstrong Bridge, Jesmond

Jesmond Dene Old Mill

The Quayside, King Street

Laing Art Gallery, John Dobson Street

Light and motion on the High Level Bridge

Lockdown view of Grey's Monument

Lockdown on Saville Row

Love locks on the High
Level Bridge

Men with Potential Selves

Modren architecture: Newcastle Helix

Monument Metro station

Moot Hall, Newcastle

Newcastle bridges

Newcastle Castle

Newcastle City Hall

Newcastle City Library

Newcastle Civic Centre posts

Newcastle Civic Centre

Newcastle Helix

Newcastle station

Newcastle Tyne Bridge and Quayside view

Night life, Eldon Square

Night on New Bridge Street

Night life in Newcastle

No. 1 Queen Street under the Tyne Bridge

Northumberland Baths

O2 Academy, Newcastle

Old chimney pots view from the Tyne Bridge

Old lamps on Grey Street

One of the many entrances to the Grainger Market

Ouseburn graffiti art

AN ANCIENT PLACE
OF LEAD AND STONE AND STEEL AND SCRAP
SLUICE GATES, WATER, TUNNELS, MUD,
CHILDREN, ARTISTS, BEASTS AND BIRDS
WHERE FUTURE GROWS
AND SHAKES ITS WINGS

Ouseburn graffiti

Ouseburn meets the Tyne

Path to the Black Gate

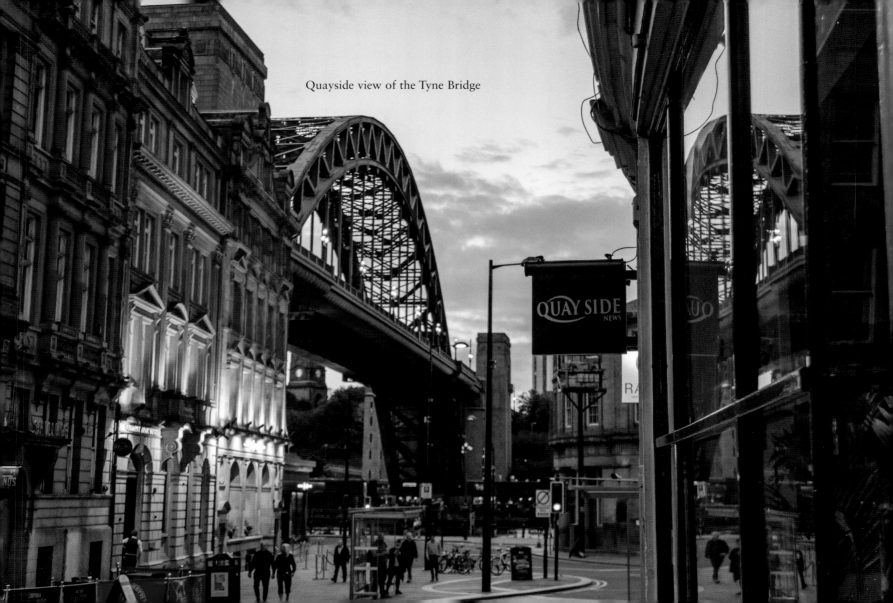

Quayside view of the Tyne Bridge

Quayside architecture

Quayside river walk reflection

Quayside river view

Quayside taxi rank

Queen Victoria statue, Newcastle

Reflections on the High Level Bridge

River God Tyne on Newcastle Civic Centre

Riverside Walk, Ouseburn

Road view of 55 Degrees North

Science Central Point

Science Central

Signpost, Ouseburn

Social distancing outside Stack Newcastle

St James' Park, home to Newcastle United Football Club

Stairs to Grainger Street

Stephenson Monument with the Okana and Vita student halls

Strawberry Place

Street view under the Tyne Bridge

Subway

Sunrise view of the Tyne Bridge

Swing Bridge

The Back Page

The Bridge Hotel

The Catalyst

The Cluny, Ouseburn

The Gate

The Old Camera Shop,
Collingwood Street

The Strawberry

The Swing Bridge and High Level Bridge crossing the Tyne

The Toffee Factory office rental, Ouseburn

The Tyne Bar, Ouseburn

Theatre Royal, Grey Street

Times Square

Tyne Bridge

Tyne Bridge night reflections on the Quayside

Tyne Bridge sunrise

Tyne Bridge sunset view from Sage Gateshead

Tyneside Cinema, Pilgrim Street

View down Blackett Street

View down John Dobson Street

View down the tracks at Central station

View from St James' Boulevard

View from the Theatre Royal, Grey Street

View of Dean Street

View of Queen Street to Sandhill

View of St James' Park from Leazes

View of St Thomas – sprawling church
with towering spires

Stack, Pilgrim Street

Cathedral Church of
St Nicholas

View of the Sage Gateshead from Newcastle Quayside

View of the Toffee Factory and
River Ouseburn

View of Tyne Bridge from the Millennium Bridge

Westgate Road

West Walls, Chinatown

Westgate Road

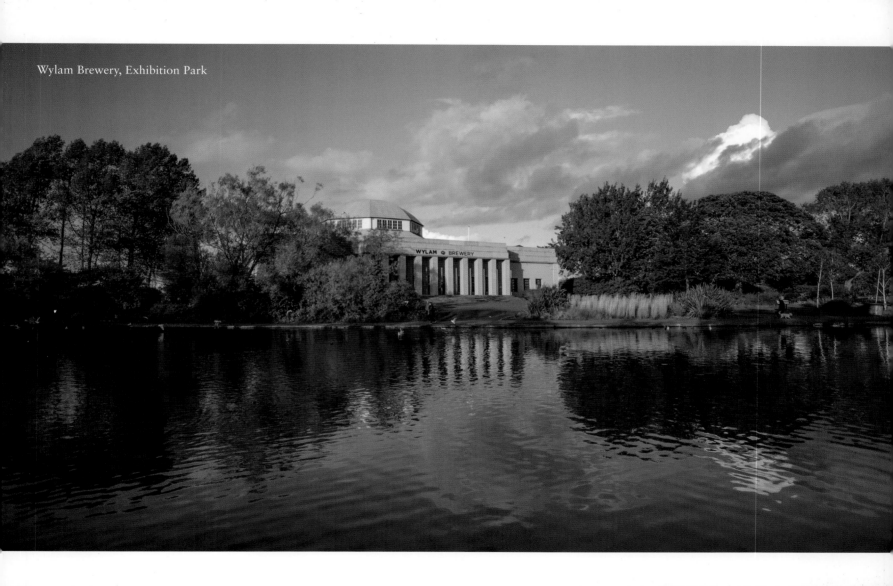

Wylam Brewery, Exhibition Park

The Last Visit